Original title:
Life Lessons from a Pretzel

Copyright © 2025 Creative Arts Management OÜ
All rights reserved.

Author: Finn Donovan
ISBN HARDBACK: 978-1-80566-080-4
ISBN PAPERBACK: 978-1-80566-375-1

Baked to Perfection

In the oven, we all twist,
Golden brown, a buttery kiss.
Sometimes we bend, just for the show,
But inside we're warm, that's how we glow.

Crunchy edges, a silly char,
Life's recipe is never too far.
Sprinkle some salt, embrace the taste,
Don't let the heat go to waste!

Shaping Our Journeys

Each turn we take, a playful loop,
Life's a dance, a marching troupe.
Knead with laughter, rise with grace,
Every twist finds its perfect place.

Roll with bumps, don't lose the fun,
Even when life feels overdone.
In every shape, a story we make,
A pretzel twist for the fun we take!

The Art of Flexibility

Sometimes we bend, sometimes we break,
Life's a twist, for giggles' sake.
Don't be rigid, embrace the bend,
It's how we learn, it's how we mend.

Floppy, floppy, sway and sway,
Join the dance, don't hesitate.
Stretch your spirit, let it flow,
In every knot, there's room to grow!

Soft Centers and Hard Truths

The outside's tough, the inside's sweet,
Life's tough lessons, all can't be beat.
Chew on wisdom, don't be shy,
Even hard truths can make you fly.

When things get rough and taste a bit bland,
Twist your fate, give it a hand.
For every bite, with laughter mixed,
In the crunch of life, feel the fix!

The Resilient Loop

In a twist of fate, we bend and sway,
Embracing flaws that come our way.
A salty laugh at life's soft spots,
Baked to perfection, we take our shots.

When the heat gets high, don't you fret,
Just rise and shine, there's no regret.
Sometimes we break, but that's okay,
We're better served in a different way.

A Crunch Above the Rest

In the crunch of life, don't lose your zest,
Chew through troubles, give it your best.
With every bite, find joy and cheer,
Savor the moments, hold them dear.

A little crunch adds flavor and fun,
A sprinkle of laughter for everyone.
Life's best dipped in sauces bold,
So grab a friend, let stories unfold!

Paths of the Pretzel

Twisted pathways, some curve and twist,
Adventures await in every gist.
Each loop a choice, each dip a chance,
Join in the journey, take a dance.

Through salty seas and sweet delight,
Navigate with warmth, not just might.
When you're tied in knots, don't despair,
There's always a way to lighten the wear.

Golden Twists of Time

In the oven of time, we rise and toast,
Golden dreams are what we love most.
Laughter bakes beneath the heat,
A recipe for joy, a warm treat.

As minutes twist, don't rush the bake,
Enjoy each turn, for goodness' sake.
In every crunch, find a smile so wide,
Life's a pretzel, let's take it in stride.

The Shape of Resilience

Twisted tight, yet standing bold,
In knots we find the tales retold.
When pressure builds, we won't break,
We'll bend just right for joy's own sake.

Life swirls with twists and turns,
The heat will rise, the passion burns.
Embrace the curve, don't fall apart,
A pretzel's charm is a sturdy heart.

Pliable Wisdom

In every twist, a lesson hides,
Flexibility is where joy resides.
When things get tough, just stretch a bit,
Or add some salt, don't you forget!

Sometimes we're crunchy, sometimes soft,
Embrace the changes, lift your loft.
Stay warm inside, don't lose your cheer,
A bit of love can bring you near.

Baked in the Sun

Under the sun, we rise and shine,
Golden brown with a taste divine.
Get toasted well, don't rush the bake,
Patience makes the best mistake.

A sunbeam hug is worth the wait,
Flip like a pretzel, it's never late.
With sprinkles of fun, let's gather round,
In laughter's warmth, we all are found.

Savoring the Crunch

With every bite, the joy's immense,
Crispy edges, let's talk sense.
Laugh at the mess, don't mind the goo,
Sometimes life's crunchy, try something new.

Dip into smiles, spread joy around,
In tasty moments, happiness found.
Together we munch, let's share a snack,
In this pretzel life, there's no going back.

Twisted Paths

In a world all tangled tight,
We learn to twist and bend just right.
Sometimes we knot, but that's okay,
Just find your way, and seize the day.

Round and round we spin with glee,
Chasing dreams like a bumblebee.
Every loop is worth the ride,
Embrace the twist, enjoy the slide.

Clear Horizons

Look beyond the salt and dough,
There's more to see as we all know.
With every bite, a chance to grin,
Open your heart, let laughter in.

Horizons wide, the future bright,
A tasty vision, what a sight!
With every crunch, a world unfolds,
New adventures, daring and bold.

Finding Balance in Every Bite

To be well-rounded is the key,
Even pretzels want to be free.
With every twist, a chance to sway,
Balance life like a gourmet tray.

Dip it low or raise it high,
Savor flavors, don't be shy.
In every bite, a dance, a cheer,
Find your balance, loud and clear.

A Snack of Resilience

When life gets tough and dough is dense,
Remember, bend, don't lose your sense.
A crunchy twist can break the mold,
Resilience is a sight to behold.

Through heat and salt, we rise up tall,
A firm foundation, no chance to fall.
Each curve we take, a little fight,
Snack on courage, day and night.

Stretching Beyond Limits

We all have dreams that stretch afar,
Just like pretzels, reach for a star.
With every twist, a fate that's ours,
Push those limits, chase your stars.

So roll it out and give a cheer,
Embrace the fun, let go your fear.
In the bending, find delight,
Stretch your spirit, hold on tight.

Twists and Turns of Existence

In a world that's shaped like dough,
We twist and turn, just go with the flow.
Bumps and bends, they make us laugh,
Take a bite, enjoy the craft.

Sometimes we're soft, just like a roll,
Other times we're hard, like a goal.
Life's a mixture of sweet and salty,
When you trip, just stand up, be balmy.

Knots of Knowledge

With every knot, we learn and grow,
Tangled thoughts, sometimes they glow.
Embrace the knots, don't pull apart,
Each twist reveals a work of art.

We're molded round, like a good snack,
Delicious tales that we unpack.
The tighter the twist, the better the taste,
So chill out, and don't let life waste.

Salted Wisdom

A sprinkle of salt adds zest to the day,
In troubles, find the humor, come what may.
When life gets tough, just chew and grin,
Remember to laugh, and let joy win.

With each bite, a lesson awaits,
Pickle your troubles, don't seal the gates.
The crunch of a pretzel, oh what a treat,
Wrap it up tight, and dance on your feet.

Crunching Through Chaos

In the middle of chaos, hear the crunch,
Pretzel thoughts whirl, let's have a munch.
Pull and twist, that's how we cope,
With munchy wisdom, we find our hope.

Amidst the frenzy, stay light and fun,
Grab a soft knot, rejoice in the run.
For every twist, there's room for cheer,
Laugh it out loud; let go of the fear.

Dough and Determination

In the bowl, I start my quest,
Flour flying, I'm a messy guest.
Twist and turn, with all my might,
I'll rise up tall, just wait for light.

Rolling pins can be my foe,
But with a smile, I bring the dough.
Sometimes flat, sometimes round,
Keep on rolling, I'm glory-bound.

The Flavor of Failure

I baked too long, it's hard as stone,
A chewy treat, I'll eat alone.
But every bite, a lesson found,
In every crunch, I hear a sound.

Salty tears mixed with the dough,
Flavors clash in a wild show.
Taste buds dance on this wild ride,
Embrace the mess, let laughter slide.

Kneading Hope

With every fold, hope's in the air,
Punching down, I cast my care.
Flour clouds and giggles blend,
Knead it well, the fun won't end.

A twist of fate, a twist of dough,
Baking dreams in a warm glow.
Laughter rises, I'm not alone,
In this kitchen, joy has grown.

The Essence of Elasticity

Like stretchy dough, I bend and sway,
Life's ups and downs come into play.
Bounce back quick from every flaw,
Wiggle-wobble, it's the law.

What matters most is the fun we share,
In every twist, show that you care.
A pretzel hug, forever tight,
In a twisty world, all feels right.

Pretzel Threads of Understanding

Twisted dough that bends with ease,
Laughing as it takes the tease.
Knot your worries, let them go,
In salty humor, wisdom flows.

Each twist and turn a little jest,
A crunchy snack, but life's a quest.
Grab a friend, share a laugh,
Together facing every path.

Hardships and Soft Bites

Doughy troubles, kneaded tight,
But with a twist, it feels just right.
Life's a snack, sometimes a crunch,
Take a pause, then munch and munch.

Heating up with trials that stretch,
A toasted life, it's quite a sketch.
Golden brown, we find our cheer,
Savoring moments, year by year.

Lessons in Every Knot

Knot by knot, we try and fail,
Yet laughter always tips the scale.
In every twist, there's joy to find,
Munch on mischief, never mind.

Each loop and swirl, a tale to share,
Of twists in fate and carefree air.
Hold close your friends, don't let them stray,
For every knot leads to buffet play.

Spiraled Embrace

Embrace the spiral, don't you fret,
In zestful twists, we have no regret.
A life well-baked may seem absurd,
   Yet joy resides in every word.

With each soft bite, the world seems bright,
   Making smiles in day and night.
A pretzel's shape, a goofy dance,
   Life's a roll, we take the chance.

The Embrace of Dough

In a bowl, I start to rise,
Twisting thoughts like buttered pies.
Kneading worries, soft and warm,
Let's roll with it, a slice of charm.

Salted dreams on a golden twist,
Baking fails I cannot resist.
Flour flying, a messy scene,
Giggles echo, oh how keen!

Each twist and turn, a lesson learned,
Like dough, my spirit's always turned.
A sprinkle here, a dash of fun,
Life's a party, we've just begun.

So grab your friends, let's make a batch,
Laughter rolls, without a catch.
In this doughy chaos, we find our glee,
Together, we're as sweet as can be.

The Journey of the Twisted

Off I go on a winding path,
With each loop, I just can't math.
Tangles and knots may come and go,
But oh what fun, I steal the show!

Wobbly steps, a dance so bright,
Like a pretzel on a Saturday night.
Some may frown, some may cheer,
But laughter's what we hold so dear.

When life gets tough, I give a twist,
Leaning into every funny mist.
With curly edges and a doughy heart,
I embrace the quirks, it's a form of art.

So let's contort and have a blast,
With each pretzel shape, we'll outlast.
It's not the straight line that we seek,
But the giggles found in every peak.

A Loop of Possibilities

Round and round, we spin with glee,
In every twist, there's more to see.
Life's like dough, it bends and curls,
Creating laughter, giving twirls.

A little butter, a dash of salt,
In every sour, I find my vault.
Rising high with endless cheer,
Each knot we make, we draw you near.

So take a chance, don't just stay flat,
Unravel the fun, imagine that!
With every loop, new friends we meet,
In this doughy world, we're hard to beat.

Let's celebrate the funny treats,
With pretzel hugs and silly beats.
In life's kitchen, we bake the best,
Join the dance, forget the rest!

Sweet & Savory Seconds

A twist and a turn, oh what a sight,
In bites of delight, life feels just right.
With sugar and salt, we dance with glee,
Embracing the flavors, just let it be.

Each crumb tells a tale, crispy and warm,
In sweet moments shared, we weather the storm.
A sprinkle of joy, a dash of fun,
With every great twist, new memories begun.

Embracing the Aroma of Change

A whiff of the dough, something's in the air,
Change comes like butter, spreading without care.
A swirl of the salty, then sweet takes the stage,
It's a flavor explosion; turn life's next page.

Pretzel can teach us to go with the flow,
When knots tie us tight, just let the heat grow.
Unravel each loop, let spontaneity reign,
In every new bend, find joy in the strain.

Lessons Creamed and Drizzled

Cream cheese on the side, let's dip with some flair,
Life's drizzles and toppings are beyond compare.
Savory mysteries wrapped snug and tight,
With each gooey bite, the future feels bright.

Laughter and cheese make all troubles flee,
Tangled like dough, yet feeling so free.
A drizzle of humor, so sweet and divine,
In every mishap, you'll find the real shine.

Golden Opportunities Wrapped

Golden and warm from the oven's embrace,
Each twist holds a treasure, a wild, silly chase.
With a crunch in your bite, adventures await,
Unroll all the goodness, it's never too late.

The knots in our lives are a comical jam,
Just munch through the chaos, who gives a damn!
In every new batch, there's magic to claim,
So grab that pretzel; it's all just a game!

The Comfort of Coils

In knots of dough, we find our way,
Twisted paths that lead to play.
Baked in warmth, a crispy crunch,
Embrace the mess, and take the plunge.

When life gets bent, just take a bite,
Chewy wisdom in every delight.
With a little salt, we taste the grin,
A twisty journey, where laughs begin.

Patterns of Perseverance

Like dough that bends but never breaks,
Each twist unveils what joy makes.
With patience learned from every fold,
We rise together, bright and bold.

From loops of struggle, we emerge,
In shapes of laughter, life will surge.
Stick around with friends, hold tight,
Baked to perfection, all feels right.

Golden Laughter

In crusty forms, the fun is found,
Golden goodies spun around.
With every crunch, a smile grows,
A crispy tale of highs and lows.

Savor the twists, embrace the weird,
Laughter pops like bubbles, cheered.
In every bite, a joke doth dance,
So take a chance, give joy a chance.

The Art of Untying

Sometimes we're tangled, lost in the maze,
But it's all part of the goofy phase.
With a bit of tug, and some gentle pulls,
We navigate the flavorful jumbles.

Untie your worries, set them free,
In knots of laughter, just be glee.
For in this twisty game we play,
The joy's in unwrapping every day.

The Dough Beneath Our Feet

Twisting paths we all must tread,
Choices made, some light, some lead.
A knot so tight, yet oh so free,
In every twist, a new decree.

Rise like dough, with laughter loud,
Roll with punches, make us proud.
Flatten out those worries tight,
Who knew dough could bring such light?

Knead those troubles, stretch them wide,
Embrace the quirks that coincide.
In every fold, a lesson learned,
For all the twisty roads we've turned.

So grab a slice of life with glee,
And dance along, just let it be.
For life's a pretzel, salty sweet,
Enjoy the crunch, savor the heat!

A Symphony of Salt

A sprinkle here, a dash of cheer,
Flavors blend, let's toast with beer!
Life can sizzle, pop and crack,
With salty bites, we're never slack.

When troubles rise like bubbling pots,
Just add some salt to loose those knots.
In salty wisdom, we find our way,
Laughing at spills that brighten the day.

So gather 'round, the table's set,
Let's share the fun, with no regret.
Each little bite brings stories old,
Together we weave, our lives unfold.

With every crunch, we join the song,
Finding harmony where we belong.
Salty smiles, it's all a whirl,
In this pretzel dance, let's twirl!

Tastes of Togetherness

In every twist, our stories blend,
A shared delight, a salty friend.
Dip into joy, let laughter rise,
In this fine mix, love never dies.

Warm and doughy, hugs bestowed,
Together we walk this winding road.
Each bite a memory, savored slow,
With every flavor, our spirits grow.

From crispy edges to soft inside,
We wrap our hearts in dough, with pride.
The circle tightens, a perfect bunch,
Life's best lessons served with lunch.

So twist and turn, let's make it grand,
In the heartiest meals, together we stand.
For every pretzel holds a tale,
In laughter's warmth, we will prevail!

Echoes of Elasticity

Life stretches out, a wondrous play,
Bouncing back to seize the day.
Elastic moments, do not bend,
Just like a pretzel, they will mend.

Twist and turn with vibrant ease,
Flexibility, the key to please.
Holding tight when things get rough,
In doughy bonds, we find our stuff.

When thoughts get tangled, take a chance,
Unravel slowly, join the dance.
The bouncing back, the squishy fun,
In every twist, our battles won!

So let your spirit twist and sway,
Like dough, adapt in every way.
For life's a game, with twists aplenty,
In every stretch, we find our plenty!

Lessons in Simplicity

A twist and a turn, how easy it seems,
In simplicity's grasp, we chase our dreams.
With salty delight, we munch and we smile,
Embrace the small joys, it's really worthwhile.

Knotting our worries, we nibble and chew,
Sometimes the straight path is much less than true.
So savor each bite, let laughter arise,
In the simplest moments, the treasure lies.

A Dance of Dough

Bouncing around like a dough on the floor,
Letting the rhythm our spirits explore.
A sprinkle of salt, a dash of pure fun,
We twist and we twirl, till the baking is done.

In floury laughter, we find our own groove,
Kneaded together, we all move and soothe.
Life's a grand dance, with each twist and bend,
With each little laugh, we create and we mend.

The Knotted Journey

Strung like a rope, through trouble we weave,
In knots we find strength, as we learn to believe.
A twist in the tale, yes, it's part of the ride,
With humor in hand, let's savor the stride.

Through ups and through downs, we're all in this fray,
Each knot tells a story, come join in the play.
So laugh at the mess, embrace the surprise,
In this knotted journey, true wisdom complies.

Ties that Bind

We're twisted together, like dough in a batch,
In friendships and laughter, we find the right catch.
The ties that we share, though sometimes so thin,
Hold strong through the journeys, let the fun begin.

A playful embrace in the chaos of life,
With a twist of our fates, we release all the strife.
So munch on the moments, like pretzels so dear,
In ties that bind us, we find what is clear.

Indulgence of Insight

A twist here, a turn there,
Spinning stories in the air.
Salted thoughts and doughy dreams,
Nourishment bursts at the seams.

Crunchy bites of savory cheer,
Teaching us to hold things dear.
Bite by bite, we learn to share,
With every twist, life seems fair.

The Comfort of Twisted Reality

In a world where things don't fit,
Embrace the knots, don't throw a fit.
Life's baked just like a snack,
Twist and turn, let's not look back.

The curves we take can lead to fun,
Doughy laughter when we run.
So take a chance, mix it up,
Like a pretzel in a cup!

Twists of Wisdom

Fold your worries, don't you fret,
The fun's in every little setback.
Knot your doubts and take a bite,
Find the joys that taste just right.

Sprinkled salt and laughter blend,
Mixing lessons to upend.
With every twist, a better view,
Who knew knots could be so true?

Knotting the Truth

Tangled paths can be delicious,
Each misstep feels auspicious.
Pretzel wisdom, soft and warm,
Embraces life, a joyful swarm.

The knotted twists hold tales to share,
Of silly falls and how to care.
So grab a bite, let's celebrate,
In this pretzel state, we elevate.

The Soft Heart Within

In a twisty world, we bend and fold,
Soft centers shine like treasures of gold.
Embrace your warmth, don't be shy,
Let your heart rise, like dough in the sky.

A sprinkle of salt, adds flavor to life,
Witty moments cut through the strife.
So twist and turn, roll with the fun,
In the end, we all come undone.

Doughy Dreams

Knead your dreams with laughter loud,
Fanciful shapes to make you proud.
Roll with the punches, rise to the cue,
Flour power shared with a crew.

A sprinkle of joy, just knead it in,
Life's a bake-off, let the fun begin!
No need for perfection, it's all a game,
So join in the fun, life's never the same.

Spirals of Connection

In spirals we dance, around and around,
Tangled together, joy tightly wound.
A twist of fate, a friends' surprise,
Life's best moments come in disguise.

Like dough that's rolled, we share and twist,
Creating bonds, that can't be missed.
So embrace your friends, let laughter flow,
In this wild ride, we all grow.

Entwined Realities

Life's a dough, with layers so vast,
Pull on a string, and have a blast.
Entangled paths, in savory cheer,
We laugh our way through, year after year.

So twist your thoughts, and laugh out loud,
Find joy in the chaos, make yourself proud.
In this pretzel world, take a spin,
With hugs and giggles, let the fun begin!

The Heartfelt Twist

In the oven's heat, we do our best,
Baking our dreams while avoiding the rest.
A twist here, a knot there, so absurd,
Yet every loop tells a story, unheard.

What seems a mess can be quite divine,
Just like a pretzel, we dance on a line.
Don't take life too serious, let laughter in,
For the best moments start with a grin.

Remnants of Resilience

Dropped on the floor and dusted with glee,
Life's little challenges, oh can't you see?
A crumb here, a crunch there, we savor the bite,
Through tasty missteps, we find our delight.

Kneaded and twisted, we go through the grind,
Embracing each knot that we leave behind.
What crumbles today can rise up tomorrow,
Keep laughing and munching, forget all your sorrow.

The Art of Reshaping

With each twist we bend, like dough in my hands,
We learn to adapt to life's quirky demands.
So many shapes, so few expectations,
A pretzel life brings sweet revelations.

Find your shape in the mayhem we face,
From loop to loop, we're a wild embrace.
Each knot brings a chuckle, a giggle, a cheer,
In this salty adventure, there's nothing to fear.

Layers of Learning

Peel back the layers, oh what do we find?
A crunchy exterior that's one of a kind.
Each bite full of flavor, a lesson in jest,
It's all in the journey, forget about the rest.

From salty beginnings to sweet ends that sway,
Life's a pretzel, come twist and play!
With laughter and joy, keep spinning around,
In every good crunch, happiness is found.

Savoring Each Twist

Bend and fold, a tasty game,
Each twist brings joy, never the same.
Take a bite, let laughter rise,
In buttery warmth, our worry flies.

Life's a snack, with salt and cheer,
Chew it up, don't wait for fear.
If it gets tangled, just laugh it out,
A pretzel's wisdom is what it's about.

Caramelized Memories

Golden brown, with a sugary glaze,
Hold those moments, through laughter's haze.
Twist the past, let sweetness flow,
In every chew, let fondness grow.

Sticky fingers and joyful grins,
Savor the bite, let the fun begin.
Mix it with laughter, don't be shy,
A caramel whirl can make spirits fly.

Woven Stories of Serendipity

Each twist tells tales of fate's delight,
Woven knots in the oven's light.
A journey shared with flavors bold,
Through every loop, adventures unfold.

Just like a pretzel, life's a dance,
Sometimes a tangle gives us a chance.
Strands intertwined, in joy we bask,
With each crunchy bite, see the fun in the task.

The Heart Within the Twists

In every knot lies a secret heart,
Bouncing joy, a tasty art.
Crack it open to find what's true,
Golden goodness, shining through.

When things get twisted, take a seat,
Laughter's the spice, oh-so sweet.
Don't fret the shape or how it bends,
For every pretzel, a story blends.

Finding Center in Chaos

In a twist of fate, we find our way,
With salty smiles, we seize the day.
Life's knots may bind, but we wear them proud,
Finding the center in the buzzing crowd.

When things get messy, just take a bend,
Like dough in hands that twist and blend.
We navigate chaos, no need to fret,
Because with each turn, we're not done yet.

In every loop, there's a giggle to share,
Embrace the madness, show that you care.
For every tumble, there's laughter to ring,
Find joy in the twists that life's dough can bring.

Bending but Not Breaking

Life's a dance, a twist and a turn,
We bend like pretzels, with much to learn.
Flexibility is the game we play,
Bouncing back with a cheery sway.

When the world feels tough and tight as a knot,
We stretch a bit more, give it all we've got.
Though the pressure may rise, don't you forget,
That bending is winning, with no regret.

So here's to the times we've wobbled around,
Like dough in the air, we spin joy abound.
We never break, just twist and reform,
Laughing at life while we dance through the storm.

Embracing the Curves

Curves are our friends, they teach us to sway,
In every contour, there's a new way to play.
Like twists in the dough, we shimmy and groove,
With every bend, we find our own move.

Unwind all your worries, let friendship take hold,
In a world full of twists, let stories be told.
We connect like pretzels, each curve brings us near,
In laughter and sharing, our joy's crystal clear.

So raise up your glass to the curves that we wear,
In this dance called living, let's show that we care.
Embrace every twist, let your spirit run free,
For we're all just dough, let's be who we're meant to be.

The Warmth of Togetherness

In a bowl of warmth, we spiral and bind,
Together like pretzels, our hearts intertwined.
With laughter as seasoning, we rise up each day,
Creating a banquet where friendship holds sway.

Sharing each moment, the twists and the bends,
With smiles our companions and humor our friends.
The warmth from the oven, where dough becomes gold,
Is the joy of togetherness, a sight to behold.

So grab a soft pretzel, let's munch side by side,
In the bubbling laughter, let's all take a ride.
For in every pretzel, there's a lesson in cheer,
The warmth of connection is what we hold dear.

The Flavor of Perspective

In twists and turns, we often find,
A sprinkle of salt, a moment unlined.
What seems like a knot is a tasty delight,
A change in view makes everything right.

Bite into joy, taste laughter anew,
Life's shape may surprise, who knew it was true?
With each little nibble, we learn to embrace,
The flavor of life is a twisting grace.

Embracing Imperfection

Kinks in the dough, oh what a sight,
A perfect pretzel? Not quite, not quite!
Yet in those little flaws, we find our way,
A lopsided smile? Bring on the play!

Each curve tells a tale, each twist a jest,
Imperfections shine, they're truly the best.
So roll with the bumps, let laughter abound,
In the world of pretzels, perfection is found.

Overcoming the Crunch

Life gives you crunch, it's a tasty affair,
Bite down with glee, savor that flare.
When faced with a challenge, don't run, take a stand,
Crunch through the troubles, you've got the command!

A crunch isn't bad, it's a sound to embrace,
Like popcorn in movies — it's all about pace.
So munch through the mess, and cheer on the way,
The crunch is just part of the grand buffet!

The Warmth of Togetherness

Gather around with those you enjoy,
Share a warm pretzel, it's bliss to deploy.
Hot and soft, each twist gets its share,
Together we laugh, pulling warmth from the air.

Belly laughs roll, with each tasty bite,
Checkered tables say it'll all be alright.
In the snuggly glow of friends by your side,
The warmth of togetherness, our ultimate pride.

A Tangled Journey

In a twist and a turn, we often find,
The knots that bind us, oh so unkind.
We laugh and we giggle, can't help but see,
The joy in the mess is where we're free.

With a roll and a flip, we tumble along,
Finding rhythm in chaos, a silly song.
We stretch and we pull, but we won't break,
In every tight curve, there's fun to make.

Sometimes we're salty, sometimes we're sweet,
A blend of experiences, a tasty treat.
Through the bends in the road, we jest and play,
Each twist is a story, come what may.

So let's raise a cheer to the tangled spree,
Embrace every knot that sets us free.
In the crazy parade of this grand buffet,
We find our way through, come join the fray!

Looping Through Challenges

A loop in the dough, oh what a sight,
It plays with our minds, but gives us delight.
When we trip on our laces and fumble around,
It's all part of the fun, let laughter abound.

Round and round we go on this merry ride,
With each twist and each bend, we find the guide.
We wobble and giggle, not taking a plea,
The dance of missteps makes you and me.

Sometimes we get stuck in a loop, oh dear,
But we find our own beat, and we shed a tear.
With good humor intact, we jump right back,
In the laughter of life, we find our track.

So next time you loop, don't frown or pout,
Just roll with the punches, that's what it's about.
For every twist holds a joy intertwined,
In the dance of the dough, true heart we find!

Flavors of Forgiveness

In a pot of boiling water, things get hot,
But each flavor's unique, give it a thought.
From spicy to sweet, it's all got its place,
Forgive and forget, it's a doughy embrace.

When friends twist apart, don't say goodbye,
Just sprinkle some salt and give it a try.
A taste of compassion can mend any tie,
With laughter and hugs, together we fly.

A pretzel's delights, they're never the same,
Each bite brings us closer; we're in this game.
In the mush of the dough, we find that we blend,
With flavors so varied, the journey won't end.

So sprinkle some grace on the knots we create,
Transforming our chaos into something great.
Through the twists of our path, let's savor our zest,
In the flavors of love, we truly are blessed!

Yielding to the Twist

Twists and bends, a wiggly fate,
Sometimes we struggle, sometimes we wait.
In the dance of the dough, we fall and we rise,
Yielding, we discover new ways to surprise.

When life's a pretzel, tight and compressed,
Just loosen the grip, that's how we're blessed.
With a laugh and a smile, we find our own clue,
In the curves and the creases, we create something new.

The road may be bumpy, the journey unclear,
But with each little twist, let's not show fear.
Hold on to the joy as we sway and entwine,
In the knots of our stories, the hearts will align.

So spin into chaos, embrace every tease,
For yielding to twists brings a sense of peace.
In the humor of life, let's dance to our tune,
A pretzel parade that ends too soon!

Conundrums of Coriander

Twisted like a thought, what to choose?
Should I meet the spice or sip the booze?
Round and round my mind does dance,
The flavor won't come from a chance.

Dare I mix it with a cake?
Or sprinkle on a bread I bake?
The earthiness will surely tease,
But might just bring me to my knees.

I ponder questions, lost in nets,
All while munching on some threats.
What goes with whom? Should I just guess?
Or simply reign this taste of mess?

So coriander, you clever weed,
Your riddles match my hungry need.
In every twist, a laugh I glean,
For life's a mix, or so it seems!

The Dough of Dreams

In the oven, visions rise,
Baking dreams beneath warm skies.
A sprinkle here, a dash of flair,
The dough will show if I dare.

Knead it gently, don't be rash,
Or you'll end up with a silly crash.
Flip the yeast, watch it expand,
Wonders form from my two hands.

What if I burn? A charred regret,
Yet all great chefs embrace the fret.
A bubbly crust, or a soggy mess,
In kitchen chaos, I confess!

So twist and turn, roll with glee,
My dough of dreams sets laughter free.
With every flop, there's triumph too,
In dough we trust, it's tried and true!

Labyrinth of Choices

A pretzel's path, a twisty road,
Every bite an uncracked code.
Should I stick with salty charm,
Or dip in cheese for extra harm?

In this maze, what should I pick?
A sweet delight, or something thick?
Cinnamon swirl or mustard spread?
Each flavor dances in my head.

Lost in loops and tangled ways,
Decisions twist through long, long days.
Shall I share or keep it mine?
A tangle of taste so divine!

But fret not 'bout this snarly plight,
With every choice, it feels so right.
For life's a snack, and all will see,
Embrace the knot – set flavours free!

Kneaded Notions

In corners of my mind, I stash,
Bright ideas begin to clash.
Like dough kneaded, thoughts combine,
Stretching far, in mess divine.

Rolling pin to flatten fears,
Laughter bursts, and so it gears.
Add a pinch of silly zest,
Baking wonders, feeling blessed.

What to fluff? What to bake?
Oh, the curiosity of this take!
Sprinkle joy, or chase the spam,
A grilled cheese with jelly jam?

So roll your worries into blobs,
Tackle life with joyful sobs.
In every knot, a story's spun,
Kneaded notions? Let's have fun!

Comfort in Curves

In twists and turns, we find our way,
Embrace the curves, don't fear the sway.
Life's a snack, with flavors wide,
Take a bite, let joy inside.

Bend a little, let laughter flow,
Savor the moments, let them glow.
Round and round, we dance with glee,
Find your comfort, just like me.

A knot can bind, but also can free,
It's all about how you choose to be.
So when it gets tough, just give a twirl,
Find that comfort in life's silly swirl.

The Sweetness of Trials

A sprinkle of salt, a dash of spice,
Embrace each challenge, it feels so nice.
Twisting paths can bring delight,
Just like caramel, served up right.

When things get tough, don't you pout,
Just gnaw at the edges, twist it out.
Each bite a lesson, warm and true,
Sweeten the sour, with a little view.

Elevate your game, don't take it raw,
There's always sweetness, just look for the flaw.
From salty struggles, joy can grow,
Life's a treat, let the sweetness flow.

Tantalizingly Tangled

Life's like string, in knots we're found,
Tangled pathways go round and round.
With every twist, discover new sights,
Laughter is golden, on trying nights.

Pull and stretch, don't be too stern,
In twists of fate, we laugh and learn.
In each little fold, joy's hiding there,
Unraveled gently, show you care.

Embrace the ties that bind and slay,
The fun entangled leads the way.
So dance with the chaos, let it ring,
Life's a pretzel, enjoy the zing!

Stretching Beyond Limits

Bend and stretch, don't shy away,
In pretzel paths, be bold, hooray!
Life's just dough, waiting to rise,
Expand your dreams, reach for the skies.

With every twist, you'll surely find,
The beauty in chaos, uniquely designed.
So roll with the punches, don't be afraid,
A little stretch can make your trade.

Get out of the box, into the fun,
Life's an adventure, a race to run.
Stretch the limits, see what's in store,
A pretzel's worth can open a door.

Whirls of Wisdom

In knots we find our little mess,
Each twist a tale, a funny guess.
To stay together takes some skill,
With laughter sprinkled like a thrill.

A salty crown for one so bold,
Crunching thoughts both warm and cold.
Don't take it straight, just bend and sway,
Embrace the curve in each new day.

Twists and Turns

Life's a dance of dips and bends,
Where every twist can make amends.
Sometimes you're baked, and that's okay,
Just rise again, come what may.

From dough to dream, we all expand,
Mixing with fate, hand in hand.
A roll through trials brings us cheer,
The knot of life will steer you clear.

Blessed by Butter

A smear of joy on every bite,
When things get tough, keep it light.
Savor the moments, spread the cheer,
With warmth and flavor, we persevere.

Butter softens during strife,
Just like the smoothness in this life.
Slip and slide but still feel free,
In every crease, hilarity!

The Bite of Truth

Sometimes you crunch, sometimes you chew,
Finding flavor in all you pursue.
The hard outside holds the fun,
And diving deep is how it's done.

Though twists may test your will to bite,
Each nibble brings a quirky light.
So munch through life with glee and grace,
For in each bite, you'll find your place.

The Balance of Crunch and Softness

In doughy depths, we twist and turn,
A blend of tough, a chance to learn.
The crunch delights, the soft embraces,
In every bite, life's sweet traces.

With each pretzel, lessons roll,
That balance brings us to our goal.
Not too hard, not too gooey,
Find that sweet spot, it's all so cheery!

So when you're faced with choices wide,
Remember soft is great, let's ride.
But don't forget the crispy cheer,
In life, a blend is always near!

Twisting paths, we laugh and munch,
In all our trials, we find our crunch.
Through knots and bends, we'll dance and shout,
With every twist, there's joy, no doubt!

Spirals of Growth

From dough to twist, we rise anew,
Each spiral brings adventures too.
With every fold, a story spun,
In every loop, we've just begun.

Life's twists are not just for the bread,
They teach us how to love and tread.
Embrace the quirky, the wild ride,
In spirals, joy cannot hide!

Knead your dreams, don't let them fade,
In each twisted shape, be unafraid.
For every knot, there's laughter's call,
Embrace the fun, and stand up tall!

So twirl with glee, and spin around,
In every twist, joy will be found.
Grab a pretzel, take a bite,
In spirals of growth, we'll take flight!

Reflections of a Twisted Soul

Look in the mirror, what do you see?
A pretzel twist, just like me!
Curled in laughter, and sometimes woe,
In every bite, our stories flow.

Embrace your shape, don't keep it dull,
Be the twist, be the fool!
In salty joy, find your heart,
Each twist's a road, a unique art.

Wobbly moments, we all share,
Spilling secrets, if you dare.
Take a moment, don't resist,
In every knot, there's joy to twist!

So rise, dear soul, with each parade,
In every twist, we're unafraid.
From soft to crunchy, we'll unite,
Reflect our joy, with every bite!

Woven Tales of Joy

Come gather 'round, let's share a tale,
Of pretzels twisted, where laughter prevails.
Soft dough hugs, and crunchy cheer,
In woven tales, we have no fear.

Through tunnels, loops, and salty dreams,
Life's a dance, or so it seems.
With each twist, stories grow,
In every turn, let laughter show.

So grab a snack, let's not delay,
In pretzel knots, we'll find our way.
The world's a feast, twist with your friends,
Woven tales of joy never end!

Celebrate quirks, embrace the fun,
As we twist and turn, we're never done.
In every corner, joy there lives,
A pretzel's heart, it always gives!

The Softness Beneath

In a world of knots and bends,
Embrace the soft, it never ends.
Life's twists may hold their grip too tight,
But softness brings the joy, the light.

With every twist, a new surprise,
Something chewy 'neath the guise.
So when you find a challenge near,
Remember soft is what we cheer.

Salted Insights

Life sprinkles salt upon our fate,
A little zest can feel first-rate.
Too much can make you pucker fast,
But moderation makes good times last.

Savor each bite, so wisely laid,
A dash of salt, the fun parade.
When troubles come, remember the taste,
Without a sprinkle, the fun's laid waste.

Crunch of Experience

Each bite reflects a lesson chewed,
Crunching through what needs renewed.
With every crack, a bit we learn,
That life is best when we take a turn.

So make it crispy, add some flair,
The crunch of life, embrace the dare.
Beneath the hardest shell, a heart,
In every bite, we play our part.

Twisted Paths to Clarity

A spiral here, a twisty plot,
Expecting smooth? Well, quite the shot!
But those winding roads bring out the best,
Clarity hides in each quirky jest.

Life's a pretzel, proud and bold,
With humor wrapped, and stories told.
So twirl and laugh, in knotty cheer,
For clarity's giggle is always near.

Chewy Challenges

I bit into a pretzel, oh so grand,
It twisted my teeth, just like a band.
Chewy and knotty, a puzzling treat,
I laugh at my struggles, with salt on my feet.

In life, we all have twists that confound,
Sometimes we tumble, sometimes we're bound.
With each chewy bite, more wisdom I gain,
Like knots in the dough, there's humor in pain.

Jokes about knapsacks and bags that won't fit,
Munching on pretzels while sharing a wit.
Embrace all the bumps, and don't take a fall,
Just laugh at the moments—who cares, after all?

So here's to the twists life throws our way,
Chewy challenges add flavor to play.
With each little knot, I grow like a tree,
And savor the journey, just munching with glee.

A Twist in Time

The clock strikes the hour, it's snack time again,
I grab a pretzel and twist like a hen.
Time does a dance, and I chuckle along,
With crunches and munches, I can't go wrong.

Oh, how it bends, this crunchy delight,
Like time that wraps round, it's a beautiful sight.
With every soft bite, I giggle a bit,
Each twist in its form, so silly and fit.

Forget all the worries, they twist just like bread,
A soft little bite will clear up your head.
In the loop of my munching, I see it all clear,
The joy in the chaos, it's tasty, my dear.

So grab all those twists that make you feel wild,
Embrace the soft knots, be forever a child.
With laughter and snacks, be merry and free,
For every twist taken—I'm just meant to be!

Shades of Salt

A sprinkle of salt on a pretzel so fine,
It dances on taste buds, a flavor divine.
With each crunchy bite, it's a salty delight,
Bringing giggles to moments, from morning to night.

Like life's little troubles, they season the plan,
A shake of good humor, it's what makes us grand.
Salt may be sharp, but it brings out the best,
In laughter's embrace, we can put it to rest.

So here's to the moments both sweet and obscene,
A sprinkle of laughter, in between the routine.
In shades of our struggles, we find the right taste,
With pretzels in hand, there's no need for haste.

Laugh lines and crunches, a savory cheer,
Each shade of salt brings us closer, my dear.
So munch on those pretzels when life gets tough,
For salty sweet laughter is always enough!

Turning Pain into Pleasure

Kneading and stretching, the dough is my foe,
But I giggle aloud as the pretzel does grow.
From rough to the smooth, it twists in a game,
Turning pain into pleasure, isn't life just the same?

I roll out the fear, and I laugh at the bends,
Every little knot just makes me more friends.
With each little twist, I find joy in the strife,
A light-hearted lesson from a snappy old life.

So here's to the moments, both crunchy and chewy,
Finding bliss in the chaos, feeling light and gooey.
With pretzels in hand, we'll savor and munch,
Turning pain into laughter, so joyfully punch!

In the journey of life, with its knots and its plays,
Let's treat every challenge as reason to praise.
For every twist taken in this salty endeavor,
We'll find a true treasure, laughing always, forever!

www.ingramcontent.com/pod-product-compliance
Lightning Source LLC
Chambersburg PA
CBHW051655160426
43209CB00004B/910